THE BEST
OF FRIENDS

Great Quotations Publishing Company
Glendale Heights, Illinois

Compiled by: Peggy Schaffer
Cover Art by: Kathy Davis
Cover Design by: Jeff Maniglia
Typeset by: Caroline Solarski and
Julie Otlewis

— —

© 1993 Great Quotations, Inc.

ISBN: 1-56245-070-0

Printed in Hong Kong

For Sherrie:
who through it all has been my
champion, conscience and guide.
Thank you.

A friend is someone
who knows all about you
and still loves you.

Friendship is what makes you think
almost as much for someone else
as you do for yourself.

We cannot tell the precise moment
when friendship is formed.
As in filling a vessel drop by drop,
there is at last a drop that makes it run over;
so in a series of kindnesses,
there is a last one
that makes the heart run over.

— Samuel Johnson

Let us be first to give a friendly sign,
to nod first, smile first, speak first
and if such a thing is necessary
forgive first.

When friends meet, hearts warm.

— Proverb

Laughter is not at all a bad beginning
for a friendship,
and it is far the best ending for one.

— Oscar Wilde

Wherever you are
it is your own friends
who make your world.

— William James

A friend may well be reckoned
the masterpiece of nature.

— Ralph Waldo Emerson

Friendship improves happiness
and abates misery
by doubling our joy
and dividing our grief.

— Addison

If I should meet thee after long years,
how should I greet thee?
With silence and tears.

— Lord Byron

It is the friends you can call up at 4 a.m. that matter.

— Marlene Dietrich

Of all the gifts
that a wise providence grants us
to make life full and happy,
friendship is the most beautiful.

— Epicurus

The best antique is an old friend.

One can do without people,
but one has need of a friend.

— Chinese Wisdom

A real friend warms you by his presence,
trusts you with his secrets,
and remembers you in his prayers.

What is a friend?
I will tell you.
It is a person with whom you dare
to be yourself.

— Frank Crane

True friends don't sympathize
with your weakness —
they help summon your strength.

Friendship without self-interest
is one of the rare
and beautiful things of life.

— James Francis Byrnes

Be slow in choosing a friend,
slower in changing.

— Benjamin Franklin

Some people have their first dollar.
The person who is really rich
is the one who still has his first friend.

Friendship is a union of spirits,
a marriage of hearts,
and the bond of thereof virtue.

— William Penn

We all live with the objective
of being happy;
our lives are all different
and yet the same.

— Anne Frank

A true friend unbosoms freely,
advises justly, assists readily,
adventures boldly, takes all patiently,
defends courageously,
and continues a friend unchangeably.

— William Penn

A true friend thinks of you
when all others
are thinking of themselves.

The only way to have a friend
is to be one.

— Emerson

A friend is one who walks in
when the rest of the world walks out.

Love is only chatter,
friends are all that matter.

Friendship is the only cement
that will hold this world together.

He who seeks a friend without a fault
remains without one.

A friend is a person
with whom I may be sincere.

— Emerson

Ｔrue friendship is like sound health,
the value of it is seldom known
until it be lost.

— Charles Caleb Colton

Do all the good you can,
By all the means you can,
In all the ways you can,
In all the places you can,
At all the times you can,
To all the people you can,
As long as ever you can.

Friendship adds a brighter radiance
to prosperity,
and lightens the burden of adversity
by dividing and sharing it.

— Cicero

A true friend is forever a friend.

Friendship is simply loving agreement
in all life's questions.

—Cicero

Friendship is the shadow at evening,
it grows until the sun of life sets.

— Jean De Lafontaine

One friend in a lifetime is much;
two are many;
three are hardly possible.

— Henry Adams

Wishing to be friends is quick work,
but friendship is a slow-ripening fruit.

— Aristotle

Friendship is a strong
and habitual inclination in two persons
to promote the good and happiness
of one another.

There's a special kind of freedom
friends enjoy.
Freedom to share innermost thoughts,
to ask a favor,
to show their true feelings.
The freedom to simply by themselves.

Friendship is like money,
easier made than kept.

— Samuel Butler

Don't walk in front of me,
I may not always follow.
Don't walk behind me,
I may not always lead.
Just walk beside me
and be my friend.

You can give without loving,
but you can never love
without giving.

Kindness in words creates confidence,
kindness in thinking creates profoundness,
kindness in giving creates love.

— Lao Tse

The way to love anything
is to realize it might be lost.

Genuine friendship is like sound health,
its value is seldom known until it is lost.

You can always tell a real friend;
when you've made a fool of yourself,
he doesn't feel you've done
a permanent job.

Friendship will not stand the strain
of very much good advice for very long.

— Robert Lynd

Happiness always looks small
while you hold it in your hands,
but let it go,
and you learn at once
how big and precious it is.

— Maxim Gorky

No road is long with good company.

— Turkish Proverb

Don't believe your friends
when they ask you to be honest with them.
All they really want
is to be maintained in the good opinion
they have of themselves.

— Albert Camus

The best mirror is an old friend.

— German Proverb

No man is wise enough by himself.

— Plautus

The friendships which last
are those wherein each friend
respects the other's dignity
to the point of not really wanting
anything from him.

— Cyril Connolly

It is one of the blessings of old friends
that you can afford to be stupid with them.

— Emerson

Real friendship is shown
in times of trouble;
prosperity is full of friends.

— Euripides

You give but little
when you give of your possessions.
It is when you give of yourself
that you truly give.

— Kahlil Gibran

Friendship is love with understanding.

True friendship comes when silence
between two people
is comfortable.

— Dave Tyson Gentry

Friends are the family you have chosen.

Platonic friendship:
The interval between the introduction
and the first kiss.

— Sophie Irene Loeb

Love demands infinitely less
than friendship.

— George Jean Nathan

I don't like to commit myself
about heaven and hell —
you see, I have friends in both places.

— Mark Twain

Instead of loving your enemies,
treat your friends a little better.

— Ed Howe

We cherish our friends
not for their ability to amuse us,
but for ours to amuse them.

— Evelyn Waugh

Do not use a hatchet to remove a fly
from your friend's forehead.

— Chinese Proverb

Friendships, like marriages,
are dependent on avoiding the unforgivable.

— John D. MacDonald

Love is a sudden blaze,
which soon decays;
Friendship is like the sun's eternal rays;
Not daily benefits exhaust the flames;
It still is giving,
and still burns the same.

— John Gay

One's friends are that part
of the human race
with which one can be human.

— George Santayana

There is no stronger bond of friendship
than a mutual enemy.

— Frankfort Moore

The essence of true friendship
is to make allowances
for another's little lapses.

— David Storey

There is nothing final between friends.

— William Jennings Bryan

Friends come and go,
but enemies accumulate.

— Thomas F. Jones, Jr.

A friend is worth ten thousand relatives.

— Euripides

The surest way to lose a friend
is to tell him something for his own good.

— Sid Ascher

The truth in friendship is to me
every bit as sacred and eternal
as marriage.

— Katherine Mansfield

Friends will be much apart.
They will respect more
each other's privacy
than their communion.

— Henry D. Thoreau

It's easy to make a friend.
What is hard is to make a stranger.

— Friendship

It is in the thirties
that we want friends.
In the forties
we know they won't save us
anymore than love did.

— F. Scott Fitzgerald

A good friend is my nearest relation.

— Thomas Fuller

Friendship, like credit,
is highest where it is not used.

— Elbert Hubbard

Howetver rare true love may be,
it is less so than true friendship.

— La Rochefoucauld

Friendship is a contract
in which we render small services
in expectation of big ones.

— Montesquieu

Hold a true friend with both your hands.

— Nigerian Proverb

God save me from my friends —
I can protect myself from my enemies.

— Proverb

Friendship either finds or makes us equals.

— Publilius Syrus

Sooner or later you've heard
what all your best friends have to say.
Then comes the tolerance of real love.

— Ned Borem

Friends do not live in harmony merely,
as some say, but in melody.

— Henry David Thoreau

Some of my best friends are children.
In fact, all of my best friends are children.

— J. D. Salinger

Grief can take care of itself,
but to get the full value of a joy
you must have somebody to divide it with.

— Mark Twain

If you have one true friend
you have more than your share.

— Thomas Fuller

It is said that love is blind.
Friendship, on the other hand,
is clairvoyant.

— Phillipe Soupault

Yes'm, old friends is always best,
'less you can catch a new one
that's fit to make an old one out of.

— Sarah Orne Jewett

Here at the frontier,
There are falling leaves.
Although my neighbors are all barbarians,
And you, you are a thousand miles away,
There are always two cups on my table.

After an acquaintance of ten minutes
many women will exchange confidences
that a man would not reveal
to a lifelong friend.

— Page Smith

Tell me who admires and loves you,
and I will tell you who you are.

I do not want people
to be very agreeable,
as it saves me the trouble
of liking them a great deal.

Friendship is far more tragic than love.
It lasts longer.

— Oscar Wilde

Each has his past shut in him
like the leaves of a book
known to him by heart;
and his friends could only read the title.

— Virginia Woolf

When people have light in themselves,
it will shine out from them.
Then we get to know each other
as we walk together in the darkness,
without needing to pass our hands
over each other's faces,
or to intrude into each other's hearts.

— Albert Schweitzer

Animals are such agreeable friends —
They ask no questions,
they pass no criticisms.

— George Eliot

One passes through the world
knowing few, if any,
of the important things
about even the people
with whom one has been...
in the closest intimacy.

— Anthony Powell

And the song from beginning to end,
I found in the heart of a friend.

If I had to choose
between betraying my country
and betraying my friend,
I hope I should have the guts
to betray my country.

— E. M. Forster

Being with you
is like walking on a very clear morning —
definitely the sensation of belonging there.

— E. B. White

I no doubt deserved my enemies,
but I don't believe I deserved my friends.

— Walt Whitman

The only thing to do
is to hug one's friends tight
and do one's job.

— Edith Wharton

Each friend represents a world in us,
a world possible not born until they arrive,
and it is only by this meeting
that a new world is born.

— Anais Nin

Friendship or love —
one must choose.
One cannot serve two masters.

— René Crevel

What is important to a relationship
is a harmony of emotional roles
and not too great a disparity
in the general level of intelligence.

— Mirra Komarovsky

Friendship is a very taxing
and arduous form of leisure activity.

— Mortimer Adler

If two people who love each other
let a single instant
wedge itself between them, it grows —
it becomes a month, a year, a century;
it becomes too late.

— Jean Giraudoux

Friends are a second existence.

— Baltasar

Friendship is unnecessary,
like philosophy, like art...
It has no survival value;
rather it is one of those things
that give value to survival.

— C. S. Lewis

The difference between friends
cannot but reinforce their friendship.

— Mao Tse-Tung

They grew to be so happy
that even when they were two
worn-out old people
they kept on...
playing together like dogs.

— Gabriel Garcia Marquez

There was nothing remote
or mysterious here —
only something private.
The only secret
was the ancient communication
between two people.

— Eudora Welty

If you want to know a person's faults,
go to those who love him.
They will not tell you,
but they know.

— Robert Louis Stevenson

Ours, that tea bag of a word
which steeps in the conditional.

— Elizabeth Hardwick

We need two kinds of acquaintances,
one to complain to,
while we boast to the others.

— Logan Pearsall Smith

Constant use had not worn ragged
the fabric of their friendship.

— Dorothy Parker

Think twice before you speak
to a friend in need.

— Ambrose Bierce

Treat your friends
as you do your pictures,
and place them in their best light.

— Jennie Jerome Churchill

Friendship is almost always
the union of a part of one mind
with a part of another;
people are friends in spots.

— George Santayana

I want a sofa, as I want a friend,
upon which I can repose familiarly.

— William Makepeace Thackeray

We tiptoed around each other
like heartbreaking new friends.

— Jack Kerouac

If we all told what we know
of one another
there would not be four friends
in the world.

— Blaise Pascal

Diamonds are a girl's best friend.

— Leo Robin

Having someone wonder where you are
when you don't come home at night
is a very old human need.

— Margaret Mead

I want everyone else I meet
in the whole world
to like me,
except the people I've already met,
handled, found inconsequential,
and forgot about.

— Joseph Heller

A friend is one who dislikes
the same people you dislike.

There are three types of friends:
those like food,
without which you can't live;
those like medicine,
which you need occasionally;
and those like an illness,
which you never want.

— Solomon Ibn Gabirol

My true friends have always given me
that supreme proof of devotion,
a spontaneous aversion
for the man I loved.

— Colette

A mile walked with a friend
contains only a hundred steps.

— Russian Proverb

If we all said to people's faces
what we say behind one another's backs,
society would be impossible.

— Honore De Balzac

If we were all given by magic
the power to read each other's thoughts,
I suppose the first effect would be
to dissolve all friendships.

— Bertrand Russell

In politics... shared hatreds
are almost always the basis
of friendships.

— Alexis De Tocqueville

The ultimate lesson all of us have to learn
is unconditional love,
which includes not only others
but ourselves as well.

— Elisabeth Kubler-Ross

Whenever I dwell for any length of time
on my own shortcomings,
they gradually begin to seem mild,
harmless, rather engaging little things,
not at all like the staring defects
in other people's characters.

— Margaret Halsey

The one important thing
I have learned over the years
is the difference
between taking one's work seriously
and taking one's self seriously.
The first is imperative
and the second is disastrous.

— Margot Fonteyn

To be meek, patient, tactful,
modest, honorable, brave,
is not to be either manly or womanly;
it is to be humane.

— Jane Harrison

That is the best —
to laugh with someone
because you both think
the same things are funny.

— Gloria Vanderbilt

Always there remain
portions of our heart
into which no one is able to enter,
invite them as we may.

— Mary Dixon Thayer

I always felt that the great high privilege,
relief and comfort of friendship
was that one had to explain nothing.

— Katherine Mansfield

Live so that your friends can defend you,
but never have to.

— Arnold H. Glasow

"Stay" is a charming word
in a friend's vocabulary.

— Louisa May Alcott

Superior people never make long visits.

— Marianne Moore

We can do no great things —
only small things with great love.

— Mother Teresa

If it's very painful
for you to criticize your friends —
you're safe in doing it.
But if you take the slightest pleasure in it —
that's the time to hold your tongue.

— Alice Duer Miller

To love is to admire with the heart;
to admire is to love with the mind.

— Gautier

When friends ask, there is no tomorrow.

— Proverb

The man who treasures his friends
is usually solid gold himself.

— Marjorie Holmes

A home-made friend wears longer
than one you buy in the market.

— Austin O'Malley

Friends are like melons;
shall I tell you why?
To find one good
you must a hundred try.

— Claude Mermet

True friends are those
seeking solitude together.

— Abel Bonnard

There is a magnet in your heart
that will attract true friends.
That magnet is unselfishness,
thinking of others first...
when you learn to live for others,
they will live for you.

Change your pleasure,
but never change your friends.

— Voltaire

Do not save your loving speeches
For your friends till they are dead;
Do not write them on their tombstones,
Speak them rather now instead.

— Anna Cummins

To your good health, old friend,
may you live for a thousand years,
and I be there to count them.

— Robert Smith Surtees

A friend is one who is willing
to endorse your bank note.
Laying down one's life is nothing
in comparison.

— Gamaliel Bradford

The feeling of friendship
is like that of being comfortably filled
with roast beef;
love, like being enlivened
with champagne.

— Samuel Johnson

Love begins with love;
and the warmest friendship
cannot change even to the coldest love.

— La Bruyére

It is a true saying
that we must eat many measures
of salt together
to be able to discharge
the functions of friendship.

— Cicero

No matter where we are
we need those friends
who trudge across
from their neighborhoods to ours.

— Stephen Peters

Wise is the person
who fortifies his life with friendship.